T0016966

Amy Remeikis is the political reporter for *The Guardian*, writing on the major political issues in Australia. During her career she has also reported on crime, the courts and the environment. She is a regular panellist on the ABC's *Insiders* program and was the inaugural nominee for the Walkley Young Journalist of the Year Award.

Writers in the *On Series*

Amy Remeikis

On Reckoning

hachette
AUSTRALIA

Published in Australia and New Zealand in 2022
by Hachette Australia
(an imprint of Hachette Australia Pty Limited)
Gadigal Country, Level 17, 207 Kent Street, Sydney NSW 2000
www.hachette.com.au

Hachette Australia acknowledges and pays our respects to the past, present
and future Traditional Owners and Custodians of Country throughout
Australia and recognises the continuation of cultural, spiritual and
educational practices of Aboriginal and Torres Strait Islander peoples. Our
head office is located on the lands of the Gadigal people of the Eora Nation.

Copyright © Amy Remeikis 2022

This book is copyright. Apart from any fair dealing for the purposes of
private study, research, criticism or review permitted under the *Copyright
Act 1968*, no part may be stored or reproduced by any process without
prior written permission. Enquiries should be made to the publisher.

A catalogue record for this
book is available from the
National Library of Australia

ISBN: 978 0 7336 4794 9 (paperback)

Cover design by Luke Causby/Blue Cork
Cover image courtesy Adobe Stock
Text design by Alice Graphics
Typeset by Kirby Jones
Printed and bound in Australia by McPherson's Printing Group

[FSC logo] MIX
Paper from
responsible sources
FSC® C001695

The paper this book is printed on is certified
against the Forest Stewardship Council®
Standards. McPherson's Printing Group
holds FSC® chain of custody certification
SA-COC-005379. FSC® promotes environmentally responsible, socially
beneficial and economically viable management of the world's forests.

To anyone who carries the cloak of trauma with them – we see you, and we believe you. You didn't deserve any of it and you didn't do anything wrong. And you're not alone.

'Jenny and I spoke last night and she said to me, "You have to think about this as a father first. What would you want to happen if it were our girls?" Jenny has a way of clarifying things, always has. And … I've reflected on that overnight, and listened to Brittany, and what she had to say…'

– Scott Morrison

Who knows where rage lives while it's dormant?

Rage, once sparked, doesn't dissipate. It transforms, it leaks, it transcends and it builds. But it doesn't disappear.

It falls out in silent tears in the shower, and flash changes in moods. An over-exuberant *fuck!* at a spilled tea. A pounding of the keys in a short text. A deep breath and a slow blink. Rage, once lit, constantly flickers. Anger is a primary emotion, an instant response. Rage is taught, the product of thousands of micro-cuts, of all those times being ignored, being dismissed. Being patted on the head and told to be a good girl. To hold the screams in, even as you're being told to speak up.

Until one day, one moment, you can't.

When I heard the Prime Minister explain that he now understood he needed to address the allegation of a rape within the walls of Parliament House because his wife had asked him to think about how he would react if it were one of his daughters making the accusation, it burst out of me. I don't know what came first – the tears, or the sound. Too guttural to be called a scream, too broken to be a roar.

It was the day after Brittany Higgins had gone public with her story. Not because she wanted Australia to witness her trauma. Telling your story puts you straight back where some part of you never stops dwelling, like tying on a cape that's always floating behind you and pulling it tighter around your neck.

Brittany Higgins could no longer pretend to be okay within a system that treated her account as a political problem to be kept under wraps and solved, rather than an all-too-common human tragedy. When Brittany told her bosses, which included a minister of the Crown, that she had allegedly been raped in Parliament House by a colleague, they didn't see a young woman struggling to put the pieces of herself back together. They saw a headline just weeks out from an election. Even then, in those first moments,

Brittany wasn't put first. It's a common theme in sexual assault and harassment allegations.

And now, twenty-four hours after her story had been publicly told, the Prime Minister of the country was addressing it, saying he'd been reminded to think of the situation as a father. His wife, Jenny, had seen Brittany's interview with Lisa Wilkinson on *The Project* and wanted to know what was being done. At that point, it was nothing. And so Scott Morrison decided he'd order a review into parliament's workplace culture. After all, he was now thinking about what happened to Brittany with the mindset of a father.

I was working – my fingers were meant to be typing the Prime Minister's words, sending them out to the millions of Australians not sitting in Parliament House, not hanging on our elected official's every word but nonetheless interested in what he had to say. But I couldn't move. I sat, not seeing beyond the darkness that impinged my vision, not hearing beyond the rushing of blood in my ears.

The Prime Minister now had 'clarity', he said. He knew the way forward, because he had been told to think of it as a father would, by his wife. What would you want to happen if it were your daughters?

I sat feeling broken, unable to draw enough breath to sob, or summon the necessary clarity to open my lungs. I highlighted his words over and over and over from the transcription feed, copied them. Placed them into notes to strip them of formatting, copied them again and entered them into my work publishing system. Control C. Control V. Control A. Control C. Control V. Over and over and over, my fingers working even as my mind tripped over the same words and circled back. Someone else's daughter. We always have to be someone else's daughter.

Then rage pushed through the numbness. I felt it, bubbling from the toes I had dug into dirt and beds, struggling to get away from the weight pressing itself upon me. It spread up calves and thighs that had been bruised by thumbs and fingers forcing unwilling muscles apart.

It burnt through my core, to the very heart of me, which had been shattered by violations thrusting me into the 'after' time, where everything looks the same and everything is completely different.

My rage is centuries old. It lived in my grandmother, when the cells which would lend part of themselves to my creation formed inside my mother as she floated in my nana's womb.

You'll find it in almost every household, workplace, street or cafe. It's in the women who sit at your boardroom tables and in your classrooms, in those who jog a little faster past you in the park, and the people who move seats on the train. It's in those who speak about nothing on the phone to their friends, so the walk to safety doesn't seem so long, or in the requests for company on a simple errand.

It's individual and it's legion. Of course, it doesn't only live in women. It's inside anyone who was once identified as vulnerable. In the overpowered, and the overwhelmed. In those marked as different, and those expected to carry a load because their existence is, and always has been, political.

That rage, that collective incandescent rage, was let loose by some clumsy words from a prime minister more concerned with the politics of the situation than the people. What had been individual seething became a chorus.

Rage never disappears. It only sits dormant. But once freed, it consumes your neurons, telling your adrenal glands to release the stress hounds – adrenaline, testosterone – to prepare you for fight.

Those words, that dismissal, the countless verbal pats on the head and the push to move on reminded all those who had come before of their own anger. It vibrated, collected. Lines were drawn between those who lived in the before time, and those who knew what the after felt like.

As the adrenaline flowed through me, I saw it echoed in the flabbergasted comments across social media. In the messages and emails. In the discussion of colleagues around me, and the heavy footsteps of those asking me if I'd heard the Prime Minister's comments.

People were preparing for a fight. Not for us, but for those who would come after us. For a political system that relies on apathy, reckonings are few and far between. But what the government, the naysayers and the journalists who still saw the world in black and white failed to take into account were the countless stories that so many women had held deep inside. Gaslights leave much in the shadows, but when they burst, their flames illuminate all that has been kept in the dark.

What the government then saw as a political bump, something to be carried away by the 24-hour news cycle, survivors saw as a call to arms.

A reckoning was brewing.

'… blokes don't get it right all the time, we all know that. But what matters is that we're desperately trying to and that's what I'm trying to do. And we will get this right. We need to focus on that…'

– Scott Morrison

I'm not sure when I first learnt to stay quiet. It's always been a part of me, like green eyes and misshaped little toes.

I know it wasn't when I was in my early twenties, when, desperately trying to reclaim my sense of self after being raped, I mistook sex for control and fell into a cycle of bad choices and worse regrets, pretending all those 'yeses' would drown out the screamed 'noes' that went ignored, dismissed. And even then, you'd wake to find your body not entirely your own. That your 'yes' transcended your unconsciousness, into parts of yourself you'd clearly said no to. 'Sorry,' they'd say. 'I woke up horny and you were just there.'

It was before then.

It might have been when I fell asleep at a 'friend's' house while watching a movie and woke to find one of his hands down my top and the other down my pants. Eyes still closed, I murmured no, trying to defuse the situation by giving him a chance to pull back. He didn't. I tried to roll over. He wouldn't let me. 'My fault,' I thought. 'I'd fallen asleep. Probably led him on. He was such a nice guy, this could only be my fault, right?' I eventually murmured another man's name. That did it. Women might not be respected, but women who belong to someone else usually are. Why else is 'no' at the bar not enough, but 'I've got a boyfriend' sends them running?

But I was almost an adult then, and I'd learnt how to stay quiet well before that.

Had it been a handful of years earlier, at fourteen, wearing my first 'adult' dress to a family wedding? I'd been so proud of the blue satin, the tiny side split that went almost halfway up my calf but well below my knee, the evening bag and shawl my mum had lent me to cover my forearms. I'd been allowed to wear mascara and lip gloss, too, and thought I'd finally arrived. Until well into the event – where, not a child, not a woman, I had stood mostly alone pretending my feet didn't hurt and that I didn't want to be uncaringly spinning around the dance floor with my younger siblings – when an older man I didn't know came and stood in front of me. His gaze ran over me in a way I didn't understand and didn't like, and when he ran his finger down my bare arm, across the satin to my chest, I recoiled. He leant forward, his alcohol-stained breath wet against my ear, said, 'You're ripening up nicely', and kissed my neck.

'Don't mind him, you're just looking very pretty,' said the man who came and dragged him away from my frozen form. 'Take it as a compliment.' When I got home I buried the dress at the back of my closet and never wore it again. But I was a teenager then, and I already knew how to stay quiet.

Was it a little before that, in primary school, at the first birthday party where the adults stayed upstairs? When older boys convinced us to play games we weren't ready for and touched us in places we didn't understand yet? When they called us 'nice cherries', and if there were any responses of 'don't' we were then labelled 'frigid'?

No, it was before then.

I don't know when I first learnt to be quiet. Probably at the same time as all little girls, and in the same way: when told to be 'a good little girl'. That if he hurt you, it meant he liked you. That boys sometimes played rough and no-one wanted to cry like a girl.

I already knew before I was eight or nine, when my dad – ruled by alcohol and insomnia and trauma and financial stress – pointed a gun at me. It was during one of his many arguments with my mother. Neither of my parents knew I had seen it. But one wall of their bedroom was lined with mirrored wardrobes, and after telling them to keep it down so they didn't wake my siblings, I turned and saw it in the reflection.

The first man I ever loved had pointed a gun in my direction. He looked at my mother as she silently sobbed and grabbed at his hand. The gun stayed where it was. I didn't react. I didn't turn back. Speaking was not an option. After all, I already knew how to stay quiet. I took measured steps down our long hallway, back to the room I shared with my sister, and spent the night thinking of where I would hide my siblings, how I would get them out of the house. I never heard the shot I was so sure was coming.

The next day we all stayed quiet. We stayed quiet for so many years, a lifetime passed. Staying quiet can save your life, but eventually, all that quiet begins to scream.

My father had spent his formative years in displaced persons camps, learning how to be quiet in the most traumatic and vicious of ways, and he carried that with him, always. When he had a family of his own, his children could never be quiet enough. And so we learnt to watch for the signs of when our fun, forgiving, generous, loving father retreated into the anger and frustration that dwelled too close to the surface, for then we needed to disappear ourselves. My mother had been raised in a house full of its own screaming silence. When it reappeared in the family she'd created too young, she passed on the lessons she'd learnt before she herself could talk.

I learnt to be quiet so well that when I needed my voice the most, the quiet drowned it.

When I was grabbed while walking to a 24-hour store and raped by a man whose face I never saw, but whose smell will never leave me, my mind flashed back to seeing the gun in the mirror. Your body can't forget trauma. It holds the sights and the scents and the sounds deep in your tissue. It remembers exactly how that particular rush of adrenaline feels, how your heart pounds in your head, how your breath catches in your throat. And while your mind rages in a haze of disbelief and confusion, your body keeps remembering. Remembering what kept you alive. It catalogues the pain, the stimuli and your environment and it weaves it through your DNA. Your body remembers everything. It's why, when left bleeding and dazed in the dirt, time becomes meaningless. You feel nothing. You can mechanically grab what's left of your clothes and stumble back to safety using muscle memory alone. You can go back to find your flatmate's shoe that you lost while digging your heels into the ground, fruitlessly fighting against someone who, at the end of the day, was simply stronger than you. You can sit in the shower and see bruises form in the shape of fingers, and marvel at the grotesque perfection of the markings. And you can never say a word for years, because your body holds your story for you.

It remembers. And it sends out its warnings. At the smell of rum on a sloppy mouth. At the feeling of someone coming up behind you. At a lover who holds you too tight, or a friend who playfully grabs your wrist. It's your past and your present and your future and it catapults you from the before into the after. Someone has taken something from you that you will never truly get back.

I will never be the girl I was before I went to buy toilet paper that night after work. She already knew how to stay quiet – but she couldn't imagine the silent shame that would settle into her marrow, and how it would change her.

So many of us live in the after, and no-one who lives here ever wishes it for anyone else.

It wasn't a monster that attacked me that night. It was a man. It's not all men, and yet, statistically, it will be a man. My story is the one we think of, but it's not the most common. Most of the stories feature men you know and trust. Men you love. We all know someone who has been sexually assaulted, or know of someone who has been, but we never seem to know the perpetrators. And yet, that's statistically impossible. Someone is carrying out these assaults; someone is creating this trauma. And it's not monsters or boogiemen, or strangers without connections. It's sons and fathers and brothers and uncles and the guy passing you on the street, or the one who won't stop sliding into your DMs. It's the nice guys who are shooting their shot, whether or not she's conscious enough to consent, the husbands who believe the marriage bed is their divine right, the boyfriend who keeps pushing until 'yes' seems the only escape. There is every chance that someone in your everyday life is someone else's monster. But we don't want to address that, because we only know *nice* guys. *Good* guys. It has to be a mistake. She just regrets it. You can't go around posting thirst traps on your Insta and not expect people to get the wrong idea.

What if it were *your* son? Suddenly, 'believe women' becomes 'believe women can lie'.

The friend who thought you wanted it, the guy at the work dinner who will swear you were into it, the boss who backed you into a corner and made it clear exactly how much of your career you were saying no to. It's the dude who starts grinding against you on the dance floor while you're out with your friends, who takes your moving away as an invitation to grab harder. It's the guy at the bar who watches you stumble as you walk, and sees a green light. It's the friend who offers to drive you home, but takes you deeper into the dark, demanding to know why you've frozen him in the friend zone.

It's the men who tell you to smile as you walk down the street, like they own and deserve your pleasant countenance. The men who sit too close on public transport, who spread their limbs like conquering forces into your space. It's the men who follow too closely as you walk down the street, hurling abuse because you looked at them wrong, were wearing something wrong, responded to them wrong.

It's the fathers who police their daughters as they would property, and the men who prowl beaches and public swimming spots like they're shopping online, using waves and crowds as excuses to brush and grab and graze.

They're the men who are all around us and yet none of us seem to know. Unless they happen to go to court – then, suddenly, they are brothers and sons and colleagues and fathers and partners and all-round upstanding nice guys who made a mistake, who acted completely out of character. Who couldn't be the person the prosecution is describing. That person sounds like a monster, and we all know monsters lurk under beds. Not in them.

It's just one more of the myths surrounding sexual violence that have landed us where we are – unable to properly talk about it. Because if we talk about victims and survivors, eventually we have to talk about the perpetrators. And they rarely look like who we want them to. Because they look like us and the people we know, and we don't want to think about that. So we try not to think about it at all.

And if we must? Well, it seems too many of us have to think about it in terms of how we'd feel if it happened to someone we loved. Because thinking of who it happens to might mean we'd have to think harder about who's doing it. And why they think they can.

> *'... there are great women and there are great*
> *men who want to do the right thing and don't*
> *want to make this a whole identity issue.'*
> — Scott Morrison

The second time I was attacked by a stranger, my body remembered. This time it raged. It raged for the girl I had been and everyone else who knew what true powerlessness was. It hissed and growled and struck. It remembered my policeman father's warnings to scratch and capture DNA, to aim for what was soft. But it also remembered enough of the person I was that it baulked at pushing too hard at eyes that were too close to mine, because even as I fought for my life, maiming another felt alien.

I'd been followed down a street as I walked home by someone who apparently liked my hair, for he grabbed it hard, and grabbed close enough to a road that I was able to see into the windows of cars driving past. And they did drive past. They drove past the scene of a woman on her back fighting a man on top of her, then on her knees on the rough path, fighting to stay in the light. I didn't feel the violence to my face that left bruises for almost two weeks after, or the deep scratches on my knees, or the pounding on the back of my head where I'd hit the ground and where hair had been pulled out as I fought to free myself. I didn't feel the insistent groping between my legs or my breasts as I strained and scratched and bucked and pulled.

My body remembered the pain and held it down, deep and away, while my mind noted information – features, shirt, height, build – collecting each data input and repeating it like a mantra. And then headlights appeared as a car drove onto the footpath. Doors opened, someone shouted, and the weight that had been holding me down was lifted.

He ran, and I was wrapped up in the hug of a woman who asked me my name and told me I was going to be okay. She and her husband picked up my belongings as I began to shake so hard my teeth rattled, and took me straight to a police station. While we waited, their kindness and concern evident in the way she held my hand and how he fetched me water I couldn't drink, they told me that, at first, thinking it was a domestic that they didn't want to get involved in, they had driven past. And then, further up the road, one of them had turned to the other and said, 'What if it were our daughter?' And they'd turned back.

They didn't mean it to sound as it did. No-one ever does. I know it's a way of connecting with other humans, of putting a familiar face on an unfamiliar situation in order to make the 'right thing to do' clear. 'What if it were our daughter?' You'd want someone to stop. You'd want someone to make it right. And so, that stranger becomes someone else's proxy and you act how you'd hope someone would act if it were your daughter lying bruised and broken and fighting on the ground. Because no-one wants their daughter to live in the 'after'.

But so many daughters have to wear someone else's face in order for something to happen. Far too often, empathy relies on imagining that terrible act against someone you know. We must protect these children, mothers, daughters, wives, sons, fathers, grandparents, aunts, husbands, uncles, because one day, it could be ours. But what if you don't look like someone's child, mother, daughter, son, wife or family? What if, in the case of gendered violence, they only had sons? Trauma doesn't have a gender, but too often, reactions to it do.

When the Prime Minister uttered those words, he wasn't speaking to me, or even probably to you. He was speaking to those men who believe that it is up to the missus to set you right on some things, because 'blokes don't always get it right'; the men who believe a girl should protect herself and watch how she dresses, but when it's a girl who looks like their daughter, well, that's just different.

The Prime Minister may only have been speaking to the men he wants to vote for him, but he was heard by everyone. He was heard by all women who have learnt to be quiet, to be good, to walk with keys in between their fingers and to text 'I'm home' the moment they step safely through their door. He was heard by all the women who had spent the past few weeks pushing against their own memories, of walking into a workplace they knew had not been safe for women just like them, of watching leaders treat rape allegations like another political issue to be solved with a glib line and a swift moving-on. He was heard by women who hadn't looked like someone's daughter, who had received no care or consideration for what had been forced upon them. He was heard by women who held second-hand scars from the stories their own daughters carried in their bones. And he was heard by women who felt they owed action to prevent someone else being one day in their place.

Being thought of as someone else's daughter is not empathy. It robs you of even more than has already been taken – not even your story is allowed to be your own, because someone is imagining you wearing another's face as you tell it. When the Prime Minister explained he knew what action to take because his wife had asked him to think about what he would want to happen if it were his daughters, something broke in me.

Challenged by Network Ten political reporter Tegan George on why he would need to think of his daughters in order to know how to act, the Prime Minister seemed genuinely confounded. 'In my own experience, being a husband and a father is central to me, [as a] human being. So I just can't follow the question you're putting,' he said.

Being a father to daughters, being a son, being a husband, being someone whose best friends are women – these are not leadership character traits. They're circumstances. And yet, the Prime Minister needed to be reminded of his circumstances in order to work out a reaction. All I heard was that I didn't matter.

My story – so universal it's heartbreaking – didn't matter. Individually, we didn't matter.

But if we were someone else's daughter, if it was someone else being hypothetically ripped from the before into the after, well, consequences would be paid. Someone else's imaginary pain was worth more than the actual screaming pain that sat deep within my sinew, that wrapped its way around my throat and caused me to wake at night, still thinking I was in the dirt, still looking for that stupid shoe. Too often, we need to be someone else's daughter before we're taken seriously.

And as a white woman, I look like the daughters of those in power. If they need to put someone else's face on mine to understand the need for action, the switch isn't a terribly difficult one for them to make. So is it any wonder why First Nations women, women of colour, trans and culturally and religiously diverse women have found it so hard to even be heard?

'One voice, your voice, and our collective voices can make a difference. We are on the precipice of a revolution whose call to action needs to be heard loud and clear.'

– Grace Tame

Women have been angry since Eve. And the responses to that anger are just as old.

We saw it play out as the Prime Minister and his government struggled to get a handle on the issues Brittany Higgins's accusations raised, held up by the swell of voices rushing in behind her.

The platitudes and the 'that's terrible, but what can we do' shrugs. The attempts to move on. The pushback and the patronising 'when will

these emotional women stop being so emotional'
sighs.

There isn't a woman alive who wouldn't
recognise the signs. In men, anger, no matter
how unreasonable, is always reasonable. At least
at first glance. In women, that same anger is
irrational – spurred by emotion, not rationality.

Men argue, women rant. Men speak with
authority, women screech like banshees. Men
were driven to it, women must have done
something. While expressing my frustration and
rage with the political response, one man asked
me in jest, 'Are you sure you're not just hormonal?'
It was a joke, made in an attempt at irony, but we
both knew it was tinged with what he believed to
be true. Women everywhere seemed to be angry,
and the usual tricks used to calm them weren't
working. You could see the frustration in the male

political leaders as they delivered well-rehearsed lines and headed down well-trodden paths of placation, only to be met with stony faces and pointed questions about actual solutions.

By the time historical rape allegations against Christian Porter were made public (allegations the former attorney-general has vigorously denied), the government's lack of response had led the resolve of women around the country to harden into steely determination. Women asked for their leaders to listen. They were told, repeatedly, to listen to how much they were not being listened to.

It's not unusual for those in power to be confused by a woman's anger. Some of the most famous of Western civilisation's myths have been built around the fall of an angry woman. Medusa, raped and betrayed, was understandably angry – and was turned into a gorgon for her troubles.

She was slayed as she slept, her powers then used against her will. Circe handled rejection so poorly she would turn suitors into swine and poison waterways. Cassandra, so beautiful she tempted a god, was then doomed to never be believed when she rejected him. Medea handled Jason's infidelity and rejection by murdering his new wife and her own children. The Greek spirit of mad rage was encapsulated by Lyssa, a woman. Clytemnestra became synonymous with being every man's worst nightmare after she murdered her husband for sacrificing their daughter. Eve has never been forgiven for mankind's first sin, tasting the forbidden fruit.

Story after story, myth after myth, women receive comeuppance for their anger and are doomed to live as monsters, cast away from friends and family, or hunted by righteous men.

Women have been angry since before they could name the emotion, but they are quickly taught to hide it. Study after study after study into anger show how women suffer professionally from displaying the emotion – while men are rewarded.

We see this played out in our personal lives, too. An angry woman is a shrew, unattractive, unlovable and in need of taming. Her voice is too shrill to be heard, her face too flushed, her eyes too full of fire to focus on. Angry women commit the greatest of feminine sins – they make themselves un-fuckable. 'It's probably why she's so angry – no-one will fuck her.' 'If you would just calm down, then we can talk.' 'Just settle, petal.' 'Calm your tits.' 'You're taking it too far.' 'Keep your hair on!'

As with so much of womanhood, anger is framed through the male gaze. Men's anger is perceived as just, while women's anger is irrational – and so, when aimed at men, is usually unjust. An angry man is credible. An angry woman is difficult. Add in other institutionalised discrimination, such as being a woman of colour, and there are more stereotypes to contend with, to silence anyone who dares to speak up, not just as a woman but as a woman who is not white. She'll often find her white 'sisters' joining the chorus to drown her out.

Girls absorb all those messages at the same time as their ABCs. Boys too. It's why women's anger has become such a trope: something men have to suffer, humour or bounce along with – but only to a point.

In her 2018 book *Rage Becomes Her: The Power of Women's Anger*, Soraya Chemaly writes how it is as children that many women 'learn to regard anger as unfeminine, unattractive, and selfish ... As girls we are not taught to acknowledge or manage our anger so much as to fear, ignore, hide and transform it ...'

Women know others will be making those assessments and work to counter them, even as they struggle to make their anger known. So it's no wonder our leaders are not used to seeing it. It's no wonder, in the instance of Brittany Higgins, that they believed platitudes and politics as usual would solve it. For the first time in a long, long while, within a long, long list of tragedies and injustices Australians should be angry about, the anger didn't seem to be dissipating. In fact, it was growing. Women were marching. They were mobilising. They were telling their stories – loudly – and they were refusing to calm down or express their anger in a more palatable way. As one woman I met in a supermarket told me, 'It's liberating to be this angry and not have to hide it.'

These were not the first angry women to speak up to their leaders. But here were a lot of straight, white women – a core constituency of the Coalition – refusing to calm down or let the matter drop.

Anger can be destructive, but it can also be transformative. Used well, it can bring about a necessary clarity, stripping back all the frosting to what lies rotten underneath. In trying to appease without offering solutions, the government found that anger only grew. And for those feeling that anger, it was cleansing. Being allowed to be angry was a positive experience for many.

'I am cognisant of all the women who continue to live in silence. The women who are faceless. The women who don't have the mobility, the confidence, or the financial means to share their truth. Those who don't see their images and stories reflected in the media, those who are sadly no longer with us. Those who have lost their sense of self-worth and are unable to break the silence, all of which is rooted in the shame and stigma of sexual assault.'

– Brittany Higgins

Just because people were angry didn't mean politicians knew what to do with it.

After his comments about the women in his life didn't quell the issue, the Prime Minister widened his view to 'all' women. In a speech to a parliamentary International Women's Day breakfast, the PM laid out his 'all women matter' mantra – women were to be respected, protected, and the issues they were raising were to be reflected on – but there was no concrete response on how any of that was to happen, and no recognition of the systemic power structures that had allowed those issues to fester. Delivered just ten days after Brittany Higgins had first come forward, it was the speech of someone hoping to put a full stop to an issue, failing to realise it had only just begun.

Respect, protect, reflect – they were all the things the government wasn't doing. The bar for the Prime Minister's International Women's Day speeches was never very high: the year before he had said he wanted to see women rise, but not at the expense of men. At a time when women needed to hear, more than ever, that the leader of their nation 'got it', the Prime Minister fell back on buzzwords that did more to enrage than inspire.

Kate Jenkins, the woman who one year earlier had provided the government with recommendations on how to better address sexual harassment at work, was at the breakfast – but it would be weeks before the government finally responded to her landmark report. Instead, we heard how women were to be respected (forty-two times), protected (nineteen times) and the situation reflected on (eleven times), all in just under fifteen minutes.

A week later, in the wake of historic rape allegations against a then unnamed senior minister of his government being made public – allegations that aired the day after his International Women's Day speech – the Prime Minister released a long-awaited response to the Aged Care royal commission. It was an attempt to reclaim the narrative. No-one could ignore the importance of the report. But no-one could ignore the allegations, either.

In a press conference where journalists were told to ask questions about a report they had been given no time to review, and only thirty minutes to prepare for, a snappish Prime Minister eventually admitted he had not read the dossier of allegations that had been sent to his office, but had asked the cabinet minister about them and received a 'categoric' denial.

'I'm not going to go into the conversation. Simply to tell you, I asked. Did I raise it? Yes, I did. And he vigorously and completely denied the allegations. So that means there is a proper process now for it to follow,' he said.

The Prime Minister referred the matter to the Australian Federal Police, an investigative body that had no jurisdiction to look into the allegations, when he knew the police had already closed the investigation upon the complainant's death. To do anything else – to allow for an independent investigation into whether or not the minister was fit to sit in Cabinet, for instance – would, apparently, undermine the rule of law.

We can't have a system in this country where allegations are simply presented, and I'm not suggesting this in this case, but we can't have a situation where the mere making of an allegation and that being publicised through the media is grounds for, you know, governments to stand people down simply on the basis of that. I mean, we have a rule of law in this country and it's appropriate that these things were referred to the Federal Police. They have been. They're the people who are competent and authorised to deal with issues of this sensitivity and this seriousness. And that is what our government has done. That is what I have done.

Morrison also said he had learnt of rumours surrounding one of his ministers months earlier, when the ABC's *Four Corners* was investigating 'the Canberra bubble', but he had not investigated any further. 'I tend to not pay attention to rumours.'

All this came just days after his International Women's Day message.

Respect, protect and reflect – but only when convenient, seemed to be the message.

Those who had been angry before became incandescent with rage. Those who hadn't been paying attention switched on. As I sat in a doctor's surgery a day later, I overheard two women engaged in a conversation about the issue. Both said they were long-term Liberal voters. Both were shocked by the lack of reaction.

'Are we just meant to move on?' one asked the other. 'Are we supposed to pretend like it never happened?'

Well, yes.

Like so much in life, when it comes to addressing sexual violence, words mean everything until they don't. The same prime minister talking about the 'rule of law' and how there was nothing he could do, had, just two years earlier, during the 2019 election campaign, spoken about 'believing women'.

> One of the early questions on rape and women being raped and the lack of reporting, and one of the things that often happens with that is, they're not believed and their stories are not believed. And it's important that their stories are believed and that they know that if they come forward, their stories will be believed.

The Prime Minister had not read the detail of the allegations levelled against his minister. He was briefed, asked the minister about it, received his 'vigorous and complete' denial and then left it 'to the proper process' – where nothing could be done. He admitted he had heard 'rumours' one of his ministers had been accused of something months earlier, but did not see it as his role at the time to investigate any further, either to find out who it pertained to or what the allegations involved. He refused to hold any independent inquiry as he was not 'a police force', despite the police investigation ending with the woman's death.

Respect, protect, reflect.

When it emerged that Linda Reynolds, Brittany Higgins's boss at the time she was allegedly raped, referred to her as a 'lying cow' after Ms Higgins went public with her story, Scott Morrison defended his minister. He said the remarks were 'not acceptable', but made sure it was known that Ms Reynolds had apologised to her staff – not Ms Higgins – for making the comment.

It was only when Ms Higgins threatened legal action that Reynolds, who was then on sick leave, apologised to her. (Reynolds maintains she didn't doubt Ms Higgins's story and instead was referring to Ms Higgins's account of the lack of support she felt after making her allegations.)

Asked by News Corp journalist Samantha Maiden why there was no holding to account of his ministers, Morrison turned it back on the media, as if the issue was that the comment had been made in an open-plan office, not that it had been made in the first place. 'I can only reflect on some of the things I hear about media rooms and the way they talk about people in those places,' he said. 'If that were the case, you'd have to clear the whole place, I suspect.'

Reynolds, Morrison said, had also been under a lot of stress. 'I'm sure that all of you have found yourself, at a time of frustration, perhaps saying things you regret. And I would simply ask you, given the comment was made in a private place, that you offer the same generosity to how you perceive something you might have said, and perhaps apply the same standard to Linda Reynolds who, at the time, was under significant stress.'

The comment was made on 15 February 2019 – the same day Ms Higgins's story went public. Not after weeks, or even days, of sustained pressure.

Respect. Protect. Reflect.

Even when the PM was trying to apologise, women seemed to cop the blame. In explaining that he had finally heard women (the thousands of women who had taken to the streets demanding someone listen had not done it, apparently – his comments in parliament gave the impression they were to be grateful that no-one was shooting at them), the Prime Minister immediately turned difficult but legitimate questions into an unsubstantiated attack on Samantha Maiden, the journalist who had broken the story that had unleashed the torrent.

When asked by the national media to explain what it was about the parliamentary culture that had created such an unequal environment, the Prime Minister, who admitted he had heard 'rumours' about one of his Cabinet ministers but hadn't followed them up because he tended not to 'listen to rumours', was in this instance happy to repeat something he'd heard (incorrectly, as it turned out) about a woman.

That, at least, led to a late-night apology on social media. Other comments were just left hanging, with no acknowledgement of how they could wound.

When describing the briefing he received from the Australian Federal Police on the allegations, the then home affairs minister Peter Dutton commented, 'I wasn't provided with the "she said/he said" details of the allegation. It was at a higher level.'

Asked at a subsequent question time if he agreed with Dutton's description, Morrison dodged the question.

Ever notice how you never hear 'he said/she said' about any other crime? You don't hear 'he said/he said' when it comes to assaults. No-one has ever characterised a burglary as 'they said/they said'. The only time the discourse ever pits two stories against each other is when a woman has raised an allegation against a man. And then it all becomes too hard, because how are we to say who is telling the truth? He said he didn't do it, so what can we do?

It's the same discourse that results in us all knowing someone, or knowing *of* someone, who has been sexually assaulted, but none of us ever seeming to know an assaulter.

We know language matters – we teach children the power of words, and why some phrases and names are hurtful. Yet, over the course of the latest national discussion, some of the most powerful people in the country repeated some of the most damaging tropes associated with sexual assault allegations.

Respect, protect, reflect. All powerful words. But nothing without action.

> *'I think we're about to be at that tipping
> point, where it will soon be more socially
> acceptable to call out behaviour, than it will to
> do things that perpetuate rape culture. And once
> we reach that, I think it will change our society
> for generations to come.'*
>
> – Chanel Contos

Is it any surprise our leaders bumble their way through talking about sexual violence and harassment of women when, as a society, we remain so uncomfortable with it, and happy for it to remain in the dark?

When Scott Morrison spoke of needing his wife's guidance, or thinking of his daughters,

or implored women to understand that blokes
sometimes just didn't get it right – but declared
that the fact that they were trying was the
important thing – or expressed that rape was bad,
and these stories were terrible, while reiterating
that no-one wanted to see this as a men's versus
women's issue, he was appealing to all those
people who were desperately uncomfortable with
the conversations they were hearing, and looking
for a way to move on.

Everyone can agree that sexual assault,
as a concept, is bad. But in reality, it's never
a cut and dried issue (even when it is). No-
one wants to think about Jack down the road
having forced himself on that girl. What about
his future? What will it do to him? He's been
doing really well at university, and didn't he
clean Bob's gutters just before the fire season?

Surely she must be making it up. Changed her mind.

People don't like having to examine their deeply held prejudices and where they come from. No-one is racist (but). No-one is a misogynist (but). People have nothing against the homeless (but). No-one is homophobic (they just don't want it shoved in their faces). There's no hatred towards the trans community (it's just about safety). There's always a but, always a justification. The truth is, we don't like examining what makes us uncomfortable, so we disguise and rearrange it in a layer-cake of platitudes and value judgements, which our leaders regurgitate and offer right back to us, on a slightly fancier platter.

You want to know where the anger came from that in 2021 sent hundreds of thousands of women into the streets, and why this time, out of all the times we should have been furious, the anger is not being dropped? It's because everyone who has ever been violated has heard all those messages. And this made them second-guess themselves. When I sat in the shower unaware of the hot water that had turned cold, scrubbing at bruises until I bled, it wasn't anger I felt, but shame. As the daughter of a cop, I was raised with cautionary tales of women who went out into the dark. How could I be so stupid?

Those messages we hear thrive on shame. You don't have to learn shame – the cousin of guilt, shame comes early. Your brain is hardwired to react to it. And so, every message you send to children is filtered through it. Boys learn women can be shamed by their bodies. Girls learn their bodies can bring shame.

By the time they are fifteen, almost two million

Australians will have experienced at least one sexual assault. In 2018–19, 97 per cent of sexual assaults in cases recorded by police were carried out by men, with the biggest cohort of offenders aged just 15–19. One in three Australian women has experienced sexual violence perpetrated by a man since turning fifteen. One in four women has experienced sexual or physical violence by a current or former partner. One in ten women has been attacked by a stranger.

But we know these figures. We hear about them every time a woman is murdered by her current or former partner (on average, once a week). And we hear the familiar 'why didn't she leave/why didn't anyone help her' refrain. When Chanel Contos started a petition calling for better consent education in schools, after she asked her Instagram followers if they had been sexually assaulted by students who attended all-boys schools (and was flooded with responses), we heard those statistics again. Girls (and it was mostly girls) were telling of the sexual assaults they had experienced at the hands of boys they knew, boys they had considered friends, before they'd turned eighteen. They had to speak in stereo before they were heard. When their male peers spoke up with a 'hey, fellas, maybe we shouldn't be doing this,' they were held up as heroes. For speaking what should be obvious. What should be the norm. You shouldn't get a cookie for telling people not to sexually assault other people. And yet, here we are.

It makes sense in the context of the latest National Community Attitudes towards Violence against Women Survey, which found declining understanding of what constituted violence against women, particularly for those aged 16–24. Two in five of the survey respondents believed women made up allegations of sexual assault as a punishment for men. One in eight believed a woman was at least partially responsible for her sexual assault if she was under the influence. Consent was found to be a grey area. And yet, teaching consent in schools is still considered to be a controversial issue. We'd rather, as a society, ignore the consequences of not heeding consent when they inevitably happen. After all, how were they to know any better? There were so many mixed signals.

We know we fail on this issue. We've been failing for decades. And when we talk about it, we mostly talk about women like me – white, educated, privileged. There have been cases before Brittany Higgins that should have sent us into the streets. While we speak of reckonings, we need to reckon with why we haven't demonstrated our outrage after we learnt the stories of First Nation women who were brutalised. Indigenous women, women of colour, trans women, culturally and linguistically diverse women and gender diverse people marched and yelled and cried alongside us – but how often do we reciprocate that support?

We fail on so many levels because there is so much about sexual assault we never want to talk about.

The stories I have heard, from women sharing their sexual assault stories for the first time, unleashing secrets they had held for more than five (in one case eight) decades because they never felt safe enough to share, to non-binary people who had been violated for just being themselves, to trans women who had been assaulted for the crime of existing – these stories would surprise no-one. We know their stories, because we know *them*. We are them. We've been them. Sexual violence transcends all the delineations we mark society with – age, race, sexuality, gender, income, location. But for the most part, an uncomfortable silence conceals them all.

So it's no surprise that our leaders flounder. And those charged with protecting us. One of the most powerful police officers in the country, NSW Police Commissioner Mick Fuller, answered the 'what can be done' question with what even he had to later admit was probably a 'terrible' idea: a consent app.

Fuller wrote of his idea for a 'check-in consent app' in an opinion piece for the *Daily Telegraph* on 18 March 2021. 'People might think that sounds ridiculous,' he wrote, 'but the idea we couldn't dance at weddings, stand in a pub or cross a state border also sounded ridiculous until the cost of inaction was considered.'

The criticism was swift – yes, it was a terrible idea. Fuller was praised by the sympathetic for trying to understand, or for 'starting a conversation', but that doesn't take into account one of the key misunderstandings surrounding consent. Consent is fluid. You can withdraw it at any time. 'Yes' to one thing does not mean 'yes' to everything. You can be coerced or forced to give consent, or at least stop resisting, and you can be assaulted when you are in no state to give or not give consent. You can be made to say 'yes', because it may be the only way you make it out alive. Flight, fight, freeze and fawn, and everything in between, are completely legitimate responses to fear, and if you are having a fear response, you're in an unsafe situation. Swiping right or left is not going to stop any of that. It will, however, be yet another tool used against victims if they ever attempt to find justice. And so few ever will. That none of that came to the mind of one of the most senior cops in Australia speaks to how consistently, and dreadfully, this issue is misunderstood at almost all levels of power.

And that misunderstanding, paired with the reluctance of our leaders to engage with these issues (how many politicians demur from talking about sexual assault allegations, citing legal proceedings – usually before any exist), eventually filters down to foster apathy and mistrust within the community at large.

In 2020, the NSW Bureau of Crime Statistics and Research reported that about 15,000 women came forward to report a sexual assault. Only

2 per cent – or about 300 – of those cases led to a guilty verdict in court.

And those were the ones that made it to court.

Commissioner Fuller himself reported that only about 10 per cent of the sexual assault allegations taken to NSW officers led to charges being laid. Of that 10 per cent taken to court, only 10 per cent would lead to a conviction.

Given that we know false reports (while they do sometimes happen) are incredibly rare, what is behind this low rate of convictions? Mostly, when it comes down to what 'she said' and 'he said', the thought of sending 'him' to prison for a possible misunderstanding about what 'she' wanted becomes incredibly difficult. Despite the overwhelming majority of assaults being carried out by men, we still see sexual assault as mostly a woman's issue. It's in how we talk about the statistics: how many women have experienced an assault, how many women have been attacked by partners. When do we ever talk about how many men perpetrate the attacks?

Would that begin to make a difference? If we were to speak about how one in three men will commit an assault instead of how one in three women will be assaulted, would the inversion of language lead to a change in the way we think about sexual assault? Why don't we report that one man a week will, on average, become a murderer, and that one in ten men will attack a stranger? If the man who holds the most powerful position in Australian politics needs to think of his daughters before responding to an allegation of a rape occurring just metres from his office, do we need to ensure the sons who have carried out attacks are placed front and centre?

> *'Anyone who twirls their moustache [and] wonders where all these noisy women have come from has somehow managed to miss that we've been their colleagues.'*
>
> – Katharine Murphy

A microcosm of society, the press gallery is filled with all the views you'd find outside the Senate hallways in which it resides, although no-one can argue it is anywhere near as diverse as the audiences it is meant to serve. When Samantha Maiden's article featuring Brittany Higgins's first interview went live, a jolt went through the gallery.

Despite what it may seem like at times, the gallery is not a monolith. It doesn't think as one entity. There is no meeting to decide how each issue will be approached. Editorial decisions are made in conjunction with bosses in head offices, but are led by political editors at the centre of each bureau.

When a story of this magnitude breaks, a number of considerations come into play – most of them legal. If we don't have the information firsthand, how can we best verify it? What can be reported from the public domain (with attribution, of course). Who will respond?

For those of us who intimately knew a variation of Brittany Higgins's trauma, it played out a little differently. Those who have been violated, who know how it feels to have all power stripped from them, tend to view the world differently. I know where my exits are. I count the people around me. I judge distances in steps, and think of ways I could zig if someone decided to zag. Once safety has been taken from you, you never truly reclaim it. Suddenly, my workplace was alleged to have been someone else's unsafe place. Nowhere is truly safe once someone decides their needs and desires override another's will. But there is a difference between knowing that as a concept and *knowing* it.

Being aware of my story, my boss Katharine Murphy did what she could to protect me from covering the story. When parliament sits, my job at *The Guardian* is to deliver the live coverage, providing a blow-by-blow account of what is happening within Parliament House and politics at large. But that first day, the blog was all but empty of references to Maiden's story. Partly for legal reasons – at that stage, we didn't know if there was a police investigation underway or how far the allegations had progressed. And partly because I'm lucky enough to have a boss who puts the health and safety of those working under her above all else. The story was covered that day, but not by me. I was numb. The rage that would break free at the Prime Minister's comments the next day was covered by ice – a technique I'd mastered as a child.

Still, the discomfort throughout the gallery was palpable. For the most part, the gallery is led by people who have spent decades covering nothing but politics. It's an intellectual exercise rather than an emotional one for many journalists (although emotions should play a bigger role, given how political decisions can have such a powerful impact on people), and at the end of the day, many switch off.

The press gallery model is probably one of the last examples, with the exception of foreign correspondents, of old-school journalism. Reporters are hundreds of kilometres from their head offices, separated from their newsrooms, covering one topic almost exclusively. The way parliament is set up, those working within it are kept inside for most of the day, with the building almost entirely self-contained. There's rarely any time to leave, and even if you did, there's almost nothing within easy walking distance. The news cycle means you're kept on the phone or behind a keyboard almost constantly throughout the day, watching the rest of the world through multiple screens that seem to outnumber people. All of this makes it easy, if you're inclined, to just concentrate on the politics, the story of the day.

And so, when Brittany Higgins's interview went live, many did. But many could not. There was a clear line between those who were treating the issue like any other story, and those who knew it was more.

Again, that is a reflection of how these issues are treated outside the building. There are those who *know*. Intuitively. Instinctively. Intimately. And those who don't. There's a before and after with any trauma. Anyone who has lived through it, or had it touch someone close to them, lives in the after. And they work to make sure others don't join them there. The press gallery was no different.

It's no wonder women reporters came to the forefront – for, as we all know, it's predominantly women who know what it's like to live in the after. That's not to say that the men didn't get it. Many men stepped back, giving women the floor. Partly because of discomfort, and partly because, on this issue, they knew the floor didn't belong to them.

The gallery has many blindspots – it's primarily white and middle class. The majority of senior roles belong to very well paid middle-aged men. But change is slowly (too slowly) washing through. Suddenly, with the Brittany Higgins story, it wasn't the male, pale and stale contingent pontificating from upon the hill. That shift created its own discomfort. Women journalists were suddenly accused of 'activism', for doing the same job they had done for years – holding power to account. The *Australian Financial Review*, in a hit piece on Samantha Maiden, named women it considered to be carrying out activism journalism, only backtracking in the face of an overwhelming 'WTF was that' from all quarters.

The shift also meant master political spinners found themselves without the power to spin. There was no talking out of this one. Comments designed as soundbites were torn apart. False narratives were exposed almost as soon as they were uttered. While this is something journalists try to do on every issue, it's often hampered by the politics of the day. Federal press conferences tend to be short, and each organisation represents a particular part of the country, so journalists are fighting to have different issues addressed. It makes follow-up questions almost impossible. But not this time. No matter where political leaders went across the country, they were repeatedly questioned on the same issue. When they returned to Canberra, there was no other issue. It was clear this wasn't just a moment; it was a movement. And those treating it as 'just another story' risked missing it. For one of the first times (outside of a leadership spill), there was an intensity of focus, led by people who *knew* what the stakes were if this was messed up. If that doesn't speak of the need for more diversity in the media landscape, who knows what will.

The only people who get to claim they don't see colour, or gender, or ethnicity, or sexuality, are people for whom it doesn't matter. It's never 'just a story'. The decisions we journalists cover have a genuine impact on people's lives. It's all real life, no matter how many $5 words it's dressed up in. And matter it does, to millions of people. Faultlines and weaknesses many try to ignore eventually become so large that even the most wilfully blind have to see. Commentators might appear on national television or write in national broadsheets espousing the 'macro' and 'micro' of the situation in defence of the 'good' guys. But it's always been about people's lives. It's a lesson all journalists, including myself, need to remember.

*'I did answer your questions, to the point
that you ground me to the ground and I
ended up in hospital but I am back here,
I am answering questions ...'*
– Linda Reynolds

Sexual assault, like every topic we don't like to talk about, seems to require human sacrifice and pain in order to be taken seriously. Or at least noticed. When we don't understand, or don't want to believe, we require people to perform their trauma. We need someone to look at in order to feel an emotional connection and empathy.

We can understand the pain of a car crash without needing to have experienced an accident ourselves. We can sympathise with robbery victims without needing to have been robbed ourselves. Same with natural disasters. Sure, we hear these stories, but we don't need to experience them in order to gain understanding. But when it comes to questions we innately feel skeptical about – like gender or race issues, or economic inequities – we seem to require our pound of flesh.

I had chosen to publicly share some of my story in a piece I wrote after a conversation I'd had with a male friend. He was struggling to understand why I didn't believe it was 'monsters' who carried out these kinds of attacks. I told him the men who had attacked me weren't monsters, they were people. People can commit monstrous acts. I also told him that, as a woman, I was more likely to be attacked by the person I shared a bed with than someone hiding under it.

I remember the shock of some of my male colleagues when my piece was published. For many, it was the first time they realised they knew a rape survivor. But we're everywhere. Statistics say I wouldn't be the only one they know.

When Brittany Higgins's story first broke, many of the men around me became awkward. No-one wants to say the wrong thing around a Rape Victim. If, in those early days, any male colleagues expressed frustration that the story wasn't moving on, or that women were being 'too sensitive' about Scott Morrison's comments, they'd realise I was there and quickly depart, suddenly remembering why the story wasn't moving on. Because there were real-life examples of the wreckage sexual assault can wrought, everywhere.

On the morning Morrison made his 'clarity' comments, a Coalition adviser immediately dismissed criticism of the Prime Minister's words as being something 'within the bubble'. The comments weren't meant for people like me – a reporter, focused on the politics – but for those 'quiet Australians' who thought in much the same way as their leader.

They apologised the following day, after reading my piece on why the Prime Minister's comments had caused such a visceral reaction in people exactly like me.

Not everyone can tell their story. And no-one has to. After everything else has been ripped away from you, your story is your own. Telling, not telling – none of it makes you any less brave, less worthy. Just putting one step in front of the other after all you've been through is more than enough. Your story belongs to no-one but you, and you don't owe it to anyone to share. If that's you, I hope you know you are loved, supported and thought of every time we have these conversations. There's no right way to do any of this. Remember that, and do what it is that works for you.

Anyone who saw Brittany Higgins in the moments before and after she stepped up on stage at the Canberra March4Justice rally witnessed the toll that speaking out can take. The media appeared to overwhelm her, the sudden onslaught of the crowd's attention almost taking her breath. Brittany carried the weight of a movement along with her own story. At just twenty-six, she had to respond to careless remarks, deliberate obfuscation and stonewalling from people who thrive in a system designed to treat human issues as political problems to be solved and then moved on from. As she detailed her experience and asked for a response from the powers that be, she was told to be patient, that the leaders who had failed her were having a hard time too, and, golly gee, to remember everyone is human. It was months before the Prime Minister ordered an investigation into allegations that members of his staff had 'backgrounded' (passed on unattributed information) against her loved ones. When the findings were released, without warning, they provided no evidence it did or did not happen. Brittany had to ask to be part of a separate inquiry into who knew what when in the Prime Minister's office. On the day it was reported Brittany was in hospital after months of sustained pressure, her former boss, Linda Reynolds, under questioning about her actions when Brittany first reported her alleged rape, accused the Labor Party of previously '[grounding] me to the ground' and sending her to hospital.

At the time, Reynolds said she had taken medical leave because of a pre-existing heart condition. Now she accused those who asked her questions of sending her there. Much like her claim that calling her former staffer a 'lying cow' was due to the 'pressure' of the situation. After all, she was only human, right?

Then there were the women who took a more sympathetic view towards the Prime Minister and government's actions, calling for calm, urging women to 'listen' to what the PM was 'really' trying to say; the ones who would take the crumbs being offered and served up as a feast. We have all come across 'crumb maidens'. These women immediately weaponise the 'sisterhood' if criticised, accusing women who questioned their stance of betraying feminism, while standing shoulder to shoulder with the patriarchal system that worked to keep them down. In case it needs to be said (again), 'women' are not a monolith, and criticising another woman for being a bit shit is not anti-feminist. Having a vagina doesn't automatically make you an ally. Morning teas and photo ops and Instagram-filtered feminism doesn't mean you include all of us – just the parts that don't make you uncomfortable, or threaten the systems that benefit you and your place within them. It's amazing how quickly crumb maidens themselves crumble when the force of the systems they have been helping to uphold suddenly turn against them.

Being 'nice' and 'working hard' and 'proving yourself' hasn't changed anything. You don't make waves by joining the boards, clubs, organisations or teams that have worked to keep you out, sideline you, or, worse, accept and then ignore you. You make waves by burning these institutions to the ground and working to create something new from the scorched earth.

Meanwhile, thousands exist in a never-ending trauma response, trying to go about their daily lives while constantly being reminded of their worst moments. The energy it takes to force down daily panic, of controlling a body where every nerve is screaming at you to run, while presenting as normal as possible a face to the world, cannot be quantified. Tears seem just a blink away, and sound has to compete with the rush of blood raging in your ears. Life doesn't stop just because yours once did. It continues, and there are jobs to be done, and people to see, and messages to share. Then there are families to care for, loved ones to reassure, and friends to check in on.

Part of my job is commentating on the issues of the day, and here was one I understood intimately. So I'd wake up, startled, at 3 am and stare at the wall until 4.30 am, then read all the day's coming developments, answer emails of those kept awake by their own midnight fears, then head into work to report on what was said. Off and on, I would appear on late-afternoon or evening news programs to give my opinions on what had happened. Then answer more emails and messages from people who had recognised something in what had been said. Then home, where I'd frantically read any coverage I'd missed. I would shake, but not speak at home. I had nothing left to say.

When concerned friends would ask me how I was, I'd answer honestly – 'exhausted'. They thought it was because of the hours I was putting in at work, and they were partly right. But it was the emotional and mental toll that wrought the most havoc. My heart would go out to those living through their own hells, and I felt a duty to use my small platform to amplify as many voices as I could. I wanted to honour their stories, *our* stories, as sensitively as possible. I played each comment over in my head, wondering how I could have said something better, been more articulate, seemed stronger, so more people might understand. I lived on three or less hours sleep a night for months, unable to quiet the voices in my mind or the fear response that pulsed in my blood. I was by no means the only one. I *am* by no means the only one. All around you, there are people making it through each day by focusing on moments. Maybe you're one. You do one thing, and then the next. Then the next. The next. Until it's a new day, and there are new moments to focus on.

Some kind souls seemed to recognise the mask, and sent notes of encouragement, or small gifts. Each one was cried over, and held tight. But of course, there was the abuse. Death threats are nothing new to anyone who pops their head over the parapet. But it is always the rape threats that seem particularly personal. Anonymous trolls wondering why anyone would bother to rape someone as ugly as me – surely I'd be desperate enough to give it away for free? Or maybe, if I didn't hate men so much, I wouldn't need to be taught a lesson. Or wishing someone would give it a third go, and this time finish the job properly. That last one came with a photo of me taken from the internet with the word 'cunt' written across it. Nothing new. But it arrived as I was miscarrying an early pregnancy (not my first – my fertility issues have been longstanding) and was completely and utterly spent.

In an attempt to reframe the issue, Scott Morrison began blaming social media as something that needed to be examined for its role in creating the culture we find ourselves in. Social media is a symptom, not a cause. Before there were terrible tweets, there were terrible letters. Messages left in lockers, desks, bags and on answering machines. All of it stemming from the same nexus – we just don't want to believe it's happening. So we take it out on those who try to remind us that it does.

And for others, again, the abuse simply stems from their hatred of us. You can feel the contempt in their messages, based on the fact that your existence is separate from theirs. Misogyny comes in many forms, and it's not just men who carry it within them. To me, that hatred arises not from hating women but from hating those who challenge male dominance. Those who push against the structures looking for equality are viewed by some as taking up space they don't deserve. It's there in the men who abuse you for turning down their advances, who respect 'I have a partner' but not 'no, thank you'. It's in those who are threatened by lesbians and trans women living their lives in a way that doesn't conform to narrow conservative views.

It's in those who speak over you, flabbergasted by the challenge to their opinions and beliefs. When a man takes a photo of you and scrawls 'cunt' across it in angry red letters, he's trying to put you back in the box he believes you belong in. Every time I'm called a nag, or a bitch, or bossy, or rude, a vixen, a temptress, ugly, fat, emotional, psycho, hard to please, superficial, a slut, a whore, a prude, a social justice warrior or, my personal favourite, a 'little girl', it's by someone who believes I've stepped too far outside my place. The easiest way to make someone step back, to stop taking up space, is to make them feel small. Your experiences don't carry as much weight when you're small. It's easier to ascribe a roar for change to 'emotion' that way. Every time someone tells their story, someone will pop up to announce they are doing it for 'attention'. What they're really saying is, 'Ignore this. Ignore them.' And we do.

No-one wants to spend time reliving their rape or trauma for our benefit and understanding. There is no money or glory in trauma. No rewards. Just a constant dread you're fucking it up and making it worse for someone else, while fighting against an invisible cape that just seems to keep getting tighter and tighter around your throat.

It's not just sexual assault survivors – it's anyone who tries to address uncomfortable truths we'd rather ignore. Reckonings don't come for free. It's always been broken people, patched back together, who pay. And pay they do, to try to make sure those coming after them will never know what it costs.

*'Take ownership of your story and free yourself
from the stigma of shame. Together, we can bring
about real, meaningful reform to the workplace
culture inside Parliament House and, hopefully,
every workplace, to ensure the next generation
of women can benefit from a safer and more
equitable Australia.'*

– Brittany Higgins

If women are full of rage, then what fills
men? Is it apathy? A lack of understanding? Or
is it an unwillingness to understand, or even
care?

How could it be that so many people have
screamed for centuries and we, their descendants

multiple times removed, recognise those same howls of rage and echo them as our own?

Why have so many male leaders who 'hear' us and proclaim belief been unable to address what is occurring beneath their very noses. In their clubs. Their workplaces. Their homes.

We live in a nation where needles placed in a handful of strawberries drew an immediate response from government. Laws were changed in a day. And yet that same leader needed his wife to draw a link from an alleged rape to his daughters before he could be nudged towards ordering a review.

And so, the rage spreads, grows, imprints. Burns. And in some cases, consumes.

It was Emily Dickinson who wrote, 'The truth must dazzle gradually. Or every man be blind'. It seems the same is true for reckonings. Tidal waves of anger rarely bring about immediate change. We know that. We are not a society that is comfortable with change – and never have been. Our history is stained with injustices and rage that took too long to be acknowledged. Pushing against structures in which the problems are systemic takes time. The patriarchy has withstood centuries of pushbacks, aided by those who benefit from its crumbs. It'll withstand this too.

But that is not to say there hasn't been change – and that there won't be more. In June 2021 in New South Wales alone, there was a 61 per cent increase in reports of sexual assault, as more people felt emboldened to come forward with their own stories. Perhaps with all the conversations and focus, they felt that their complaints would be taken seriously. Or they were just tired of staying silent.

Sunlight is slowly breaking through some of the thickest clouds that have surrounded our most powerful institutions and, despite the attempts to placate, people have refused to stay quiet. It's a start.

But this is not a 'women's issue' and it is not for women to solve. Women are pushed to the forefront to address the issue, to speak on something that by and large is happening *to* them, not *by* them. There is a danger of putting people on pedestals and expecting them to solve all our issues, or speak on behalf of everyone. No-one can. Despite the universality of the experience, it is still intensely individual. My experiences as a white woman do not come with the same challenges as those of an Indigenous woman, a woman of colour, a trans person or anyone who lives in a different part of the binary than I do. Economics makes a massive difference. So do cultural attitudes to women and sex.

Speaking out takes its toll. All around us, people are staying silent because it's the safer choice. Our job is to clear space and listen to all the stories – and hear what's not being said in the silences. And to push for men to start acting. Hell, push for men to start getting uncomfortable! It doesn't matter if it's 'not all men'. No-one is saying it is. But it's certainly *enough* men. When talking about someone being assaulted in a bar or club – another crime primarily carried out by (and targeting) men – no-one assumes you mean 'all men'. And yet it's become an instinctual response when conversations of sexual assault, harassment and consent begin to take hold.

If the age-old playground refrain 'he only does it because he likes you' is starting to be challenged, why do we still joke about the 'friend zone'? Is the worst thing a man can experience really that a woman only likes his companionship and doesn't want to sleep with him? Why do we fuck-zone all women? Why must we assume all interactions between men and women could end with sex? These harmless sayings help create a culture in which someone saying 'no' could probably mean 'yes' if you just keep pushing. Or maybe you just take it. After all, isn't it what you're owed?

In order to achieve real change, more than half the population needs to give a shit. And we all need to give a shit about *all* of it – not just when it looks like us or someone we know.

Which means changing attitudes from the ground up. And that will take generations.

Rage can propel you further than you thought possible. Anger can be healing. It strips away all of those niceties that kept you quiet, that made you accept the unacceptable. When embraced, it can be productive, sending you out into the streets, impelling you to stand against systems that were built to keep you down.

But rage can never truly be satisfied. There are always going to be new battles. None of us are equal until all of us are. There is always going to be something that needs a bigger push. Change seems glacial, and in the end, those who hold the power find ways to set new rules that continue to ensure their own comfort.

Respect, protect, reflect in the hands of an unwilling leadership becomes nod, deflect, placate. Reviews are only as strong as the action around them. And we all know 'blokes don't always get it right'. Well, neither do their wives, it seems. The thing about reckonings is that for them to truly occur, all that came before has to be burnt to the ground. And there are a lot of people quite happy with the way in which things are standing in the way of that happening. Then there is the matter of what is rebuilt from the ashes. Things can't be built in the image of what we already know. Which means facing some uncomfortable truths of our own.

From where we stand right now, it's obvious that there is a long way to go. There are still attempts to deflect from the issue, while others have tried and will continue to try to hijack the momentum for their own comfort. But there has been a shift. All around us, people are standing ready to fight. Some quietly, some with lighters in hands, others with flamethrowers. All share the same goal: to ensure no-one else has to live with the trauma and rage they do. And if that's not worth fighting for, I don't know what is.

Because the only thing worse than living with this yourself is wondering if someone close to you could be next.

And how would you feel if you only acted because, one day, it was your daughter.

Acknowledgements

To all those who have helped me carry my load – I can never thank you enough. I love you all. Take care of you.

All of the thank yous to Louise Adler and Hachette, who believed in this project well before anyone, including me, and to Jacquie Brown and her generous team who helped guide me through the white-hot rage to forming words on a page.

Notes

Jenny and I spoke last night (p. 1) https://www.pm.gov.
au/media/doorstop-interview-australian-parliament-
house-act-160221

... blokes don't get it right (p. 10) https://www.pm.gov.
au/media/interview-ray-hadley-2gb-5

... there are great women (p.24) https://www.pm.gov.
au/media/interview-ray-hadley-2gb-5

One voice, your voice (p. 33) https://www.theguardian.
com/commentisfree/2021/mar/04/share-your-truth-
it-is-your-power-grace-tames-address-to-the-national-
press-club

I am cognisant of (p. 41) https://www.abc.net.au/
news/2021-03-15/brittany-higgins-speech-womens-
march-parliament-house-canberra/13248908

We can't have a situation (p. 45) https://www.pm.gov.
au/media/press-conference-kirribilli-nsw-2

One of the early questions (p. 48) https://twitter.com/
samanthamaiden/status/1366304759871729666?ref_sr
c=twsrc%5Etfw%7Ctwcamp%5Etweetembed%7C
twterm%5E1366304759871729666%7Ctwgr%5E%7
Ctwcon%5Es1_&ref_url=https%3A%2F%2Fwww.
theguardian.com%2Faustralia-news%2F2021%
2Fmar%2F03%2Fgrace-tame-chides-scott-morrison-
for-his-handling-of-sexual-assault-claims

I can only reflect (p. 50) https://www.pm.gov.au/
media/press-conference-sydney-nsw-7

I'm sure that all (p. 51) https://www.youtube.com/
watch?v=QxqDETrC8Mg

I think we're about to (p. 55) https://www.smh.com.
au/national/it-started-on-instagram-now-chanels-petition-is-leading-a-sex-education-revolution-
20210305-p5780k.html

By the time they are fifteen (p. 58) 'Sexual assault in
Australia', Australian Institute of Health and Welfare,
28 August 2020. Cat. no. FDV 5. https://www.aihw.
gov.au/reports/domesticviolence/sexual-assault-in-
australia/contents/summary

It makes sense in the (p. 60) 'Young Australians'
attitudes to violence against women and gender
equality: Findings from the 2017 National Community
Attitudes towards Violence against Women Survey
(NCAS)', Politoff, V., Crabbe, M., Honey, N., Mannix,
S., Mickle, J., Morgan, J., Parkes, A., Powell, A.,
Stubbs, J., Ward, A., and Webster, K. ANROWS
Insights, Issue 01/2019.

In 2020, the NSW Bureau (p. 65) https://www.bocsar.
nsw.gov.au/Pages/bocsar_pages/Sexual-assault.aspx

Commissioner Fuller himself reported (p. 66)
'Sexual assault in Australia', Australian Institute of
Health and Welfare, 28 August 2020. Cat. no. FDV 5.

https://www.aihw.gov.au/reports/domestic-violence/
sexual-assault-in-australia/contents/summary

Anyone who twirls their (p. 68) https://twitter.com/
murpharoo/status/1377175312480358407?s=20

I did answer your questions (p. 78) https://parlinfo.
aph.gov.au/parlInfo/download/committees/
estimate/894056b6–85c9–409a-9c50–055086af782e/
toc_pdf/Community%20Affairs%20Legislation%20
Committee_2021_06_04_8840_Official.pdf;fi
leType=application%2Fpdf#search=%22com
mittees/estimate/894056b6–85c9–409a-9c50–
055086af782e/0000%22

Take ownership of your (p. 94) https://www.abc.net.
au/news/2021-03-15/brittany-higgins-speech-womens-
march-parliament-house-canberra/13248908

In June 2021 (p. 96) 'Sexual assault reports to police
spiked 61% in March following public reckoning',
Hunter, F. and Chrysanthos, N., 10 June 2021.
https://www.smh.com.au/national/nsw/sexualassault-
reports-to-police-spiked-61-percent-inmarch-
following-public-reckoning-20210610